MRS. TILLIE (PIERCE) ALLEMAN
At the time of the Battle of Gettysburg
(Adams County Historical Society)

THE NATIONAL MONUMENT AT GETTYSBURG.

AT GETTYSBURG

OR

What a Girl Saw and Heard
of the Battle.

A TRUE NARRATIVE.

BY

MRS. TILLIE (PIERCE) ALLEMAN.

NEW YORK,
W. LAKE BORLAND,
1889.

Reprinted and distributed by:

Butternut and Blue
3411 Northwind Road
Baltimore, MD. 21234
(410) 256-9220
and
Stan Clark Military Books
915 Fairview Avenue
Gettysburg, PA. 17325
(717) 337-1728

ISBN: 1-879664-20-8

INTRODUCTION

Roughly eighty eyewitness accounts of the Battle of Gettysburg are known to have been written by local Gettysburg residents during the days, years, and decades following the great events of July 1-3, 1863. Without question, among the most outstanding of these was the account written by Tillie Pierce Alleman, AT GETTYSBURG: OR WHAT A GIRL SAW AND HEARD OF THE BATTLE, A TRUE NARRATIVE, published privately in 1888. So scarce is this booklet today that only a handful of original copies are currently known to exist.

Since my first exposure to the Tillie Pierce Alleman account nearly twenty years ago, when I was in the midst of researching GETTYSBURG: A JOURNEY IN TIME, I have come to learn a great deal more about the community of Gettysburg during the war, including Tillie Pierce, her family, and her neighbors. It therefore gives me great pleasure to herein share some of the fruits of my labors with the readers of this volume.

Matilda (Tillie) J. Pierce, daughter of James and Margaret Pierce, was born in Gettysburg about 1848. She was listed as age 12 in the 1860 census and was consequently about 15 at the time of the battle in July 1863. Her father, James, was a butcher by trade, and although not a wealthy man, the local tax and census records indicate that the

Pierce family lived in comparative financial comfort. Aged 55 in 1863, James had long involved himself in community affairs, being an active members of the Methodist Church on East Middle Street, the Gettysburg Temperance Society, the Citizens Band of Gettysburg, and the Gettys Lodge of the Odd Fellows.

In 1835, James Pierce married Miss Margaret McCurdy of Gettysburg and the couple eventually had four children, all of whom were living at home on the eve of the Civil War. According to the 1860 census records, the two eldest, James Shaw (24) and William H. (19), worked with their father in the butcher shop; the two youngest, Margaret A. (14) and Matilda (12), both attended school, obviously in town. By the time of the battle, the two Pierce sons were serving in the Union army: Private James Shaw Pierce with Company K, 1st Regiment, Pennsylvania Reserves, Army of the Potomac; and Private William H. Pierce, Company E, 15th Pennsylvania Cavalry, Army of the Cumberland. Both survived the war.

The Pierce residence, as well as the family butcher shop, was situated on the southwest corner of South Baltimore Street and Breckenridge Street. The orginal two-and-a-half-story brick dwelling still stands today at 301-303 Baltimore Street.

With the advent of war in 1861, Mrs. Margaret Pierce also became involved in community affairs, serving as a manager of the Ladies Union Relief Society of Gettysburg, a group dedicated to alleviating the needs of the local soldiers at the front.

By July 1863, Tillie was attending the "Young Ladies Seminary" in Gettysburg, located at the southeast corner of High Street and Washington Street. The institute was a finishing school for girls, most of whom were local and many of whom came from the "better" families in town. The school was operated by Mrs. Rebecca Eyster, widow of the institute's founder, Reverend David Eyster, who had died in 1861. During the war Mrs. Eyster served as the president of the Ladies Union Relief Society and was undoubtedly well acquainted with Tillie's mother. The original "Seminary" building still stands at 66-68 West High Street.

Being for the most part an eyewitness account of the battle by a literate and educated person, Tillie's reminiscence, not surprisingly, withstands historical scrutiny well. Much of what she describes can be corroborated by independent sources, and the credibility of her own experiences in particular can be considered especially sound. The only area of her account where a historian would do well to be extremely cautious is the section where Tillie claimed to have witnessed, from the Jacob Weikert house, actual infantry fighting east of Little Round Top. She described, for example, the charge of the Pennsylvania Reserves on July 2, 1863, which took place on the other side of Little Round Top. Unless she witnessed something that has not been recorded elsewhere, it is inconceivable that anyone positioned at the Weikert house, as Tillie was, could have seen the charge.

A probable explanation for this apparent discrepancy on Tillie's part is her mention later (page 80) that she toured the scene of action on July 5th with Beckie Weikert and Lieutenant George Kitzmiller of her brother James' Company K, 1st Reserves. Lieutenant Kitzmiller was in fact a participant in the charge down the western slope of Little Round Top on July 2nd, and it is probable that Tillie, either inadvertently or for whatever reason, incorporated Kitzmiller's description into her own eyewitness account of the events of that day.

But aside from such possible lapses in memory, Tillie's account exudes credibility. Of particular interest is the incident concerning the young boy, Sam, who lived with the Pierce family in 1863, and Sam's purposely unnamed sister who so irritated Tillie on June 26th (pages 26-27). The boy was Samuel S. Wade, then about 12 or 13, and his sister was none other than Mary Virginia

(Jennie) Wade, who was killed by a stray bullet on July 3rd to become an instant, as well as locally controversial heroine.

Frequently referred to in Tillie's account was Mrs. Schriver, a neighbor of the Pierces' who took Tillie with her to her father's home, the Jacob Weikert farm, on July 1st. Henrietta Weikert Schriver, aged about 25 in 1863, was the wife of Sergeant George W. Schriver who was then serving in Co. C of Cole's Maryland Cavalry. Formed in 1861, Cole's Cavalry included a number of men from Adams County, Pennsylvania.

Accompanying Mrs. Schriver and Tillie to the Weikert farm were the two Schriver children, Sarah L. and Mary M., age 7 and 6 respectively in 1863. The Schriver's brick home in Gettysburg is still standing at 309-311 Baltimore Street. Another brick dwelling, currently (and incorrectly) bearing an 1863 plaque, today occupied what was as late as 1872 a half-lot space between the Schriver and Pierce homes. Interestingly enough, local records indicate that a ten-pin bowling alley extended from the rear of the Schriver property (mentioned on pg. 113), and it may be presumed that George Schriver was the proprietor, or at least rented the bowling alley to someone else.

Not mentioned in Tillie's narrative was the fact that Henrietta's husband, Sergeant George W. Schriver, was captured during a cavalry skirmish in Virginia on New Year's Day, 1864, and subsequently died at Andersonville Prison on August 27th of that same year.

The Jacob Weikert Farmhouse on the Taneytown Road, although today privately owned, still appears much as it did at the time of the battle. The residents listed there in the 1860 census included Jacob, then aged 63, his wife Sarah, 58, their two youngest children, Rebecca (Beckie), 16, David, 11, as well as one of Jacob's adult sons and his family.

Likewise still standing today, albeit with a later brick facade (ca. 1910), is the old Methodist parsonage directly across Baltimore Street from the Pierce residence. Occupied by Reverend George Bergstresser in 1863, the building still holds the replacement artillery projectile, mentioned on page 97, to the right of the righthand second-story window. The structure is today 304 Baltimore Street.

On September 28, 1871, at Christ Lutheran Church in Gettysburg, Tillie Pierce married Harrisburg native, Horace P. Alleman, an 1869 graduate of Pennsylvania (Gettysburg) College. Horace Alleman, who had briefly served in the 30th Pennsylvania Emergency Militia in 1863, practiced law in Selinsgrove, Pennsylvania, from 1871 until his death in 1908. The couple had three children, Harry P., Mary, and Anna. Tillie died in 1914 and was buried in the Trinity Lutheran Cemetery at Selinsgrove.

Although Tillie Pierce Alleman's account of the Battle of Gettysburg was written twenty-five years after the event, it remains a classic in the truest sense of the word, and will long provide scholars with a treasure-trove of detail to be examined and analyzed well into the future--or as long as at least one person remains who is concerned about "what a girl saw and heard of the battle."

William A. Frassanito
Gettysburg, Pennsylvania
February 1987

CONTENTS.

CHAPTER I INTRODUCTION.

"   II INCIDENTS PRECEDING THE BATTLE.

"   III DURING THE FIRST DAY OF THE BATTLE.

"   IV DURING THE SECOND DAY OF THE BATTLE.

"   V DURING THE THIRD DAY OF THE BATTLE.

"   VI AFTER THE BATTLE.

"   VII HOME.

"   VIII CONCLUSION.

ILLUSTRATIONS.

1 MAP OF THE FIRST DAY'S BATTLE.

2 FLEEING FROM DANGER.

3 MAP OF THE SECOND DAY'S BATTLE.

4 CHARGE OF THE PENNSLYVANIA RESERVES,

5 MAP OF THE THIRD DAY'S BATTLE.

PREFACE.

The experience of a little girl, during three days of a hard fought battle, as portrayed in this volume is certainly of rare occurrence, and very likely has never been realized before.

Such a narrative as the following, is worthy of preservation among the pages of our nations literature.

The story is told with such marked faithfulness, such honesty of expression, such vividness of portrayal, that those who lived in, and passed through those scenes, or similar ones, will at once recognize the situations, and surroundings, as natural and real.

While perusing its pages, the veteran will again live in the days gone by; when he tramped the dusty march, joined in the terrible charge, or suffered in the army hospital.

The Heroine of this book, performed her part well; but it is doubtful whether, at the time, she fully realized the heart-felt thanks, and noble thoughts that sprang from the "Boys in Blue," in response to her heroism and kindness.

How vividly is presented the weary march to the field of conflict; our eagerness to quaff the sparkling water, as she handed it to us, fresh from the cooling spring.

We thanked her, but she did not hear the full gratitude that was in our hearts.

Who but a soldier can know the welling emotions in that dying general's breast, when, perhaps for the first time in many months, he gazed into an innocent and child-like face, seeing naught but tender love and deep sympathy.

Did she not in part, take the place of those near and dear to his heart, but who, on that fearful night were many miles away? How his thoughts must have flashed homeward!

And oh! the tender chords that must have been touched in his valiant soul! No wonder he looked "so earnestly" in her face. He was feasting on the sympathies that sprang from her heart and illumined her countenance.

She did greater things than she knew, and her reward will follow.

But we shall refer to no more scenes. They are many and varied. In their contemplation, the reader will experience his own thoughts and emotions.

We have been asked to write a preface to her narrative; but we cannot slight this opportunity of thanking her in the name of the "Boys in Blue," and all patriots, for what she did.

We are truly glad to have this touching and thrilling story of her experience at the battle of Gettysburg, even though after many years; and our only regret is, that many of our comrades have answered to the last roll-call, before its publication.

We will rejoice in its publication, and wide circulation; for it is deserving a welcome, not only in public libraries, but in the family circle of every American.

It cannot fail to interest and instruct both old and young.

The book will speak for itself.

A VETERAN.

"AT GETTYSBURG."

CHAPTER I.

INTRODUCTION.

Impressed with the fact that incidents connected with the Battle of Gettysburg, are daily becoming more appreciated, and believing that the recital of those occurrences will awaken new interest as time rolls on, I am constrained to transmit in some tangible form, my knowledge of the place now so historic, as well as my experience during those thrilling days of July, 1863.

Nor is it with any desire to be classed among the heroines of that period, that these lines are written ; but simply to show what many a patriotic and loyal girl would have done if surrounded by similar circumstances.

In truth, the history of those days contains numerous instances, in which America's daughters, loyal to their country and flag, have experienced, suffered and sacrificed far more than did the present writer.

In their behalf, and as a legacy to my own off-spring, I therefore pen these lines, and deem it un-necessary to make any further apology.

————

Gettysburg is my native place.

As is doubtless known to many of my readers, it is most pleasantly located in a healthful region of country, near the southern border of Pennsylvania.

Prior to the battle it was comparatively unknown to the outside world, save to those interested in the Lutheran College and Theological Seminary here located.

From year to year it pursued the even and quiet tenor of an inland town, with nothing to vary the monotony but the annual exercises of the above-named institutions.

On these occasions the influx of strangers, for the short period of commencement week, did add some stir and life to the place, but only to have it settle into more irksome quietude after the visitors and their dear boys had left.

To-day Gettysburg is a changed place. A new spirit and enterprise have taken hold of its inhabtants, and evidences of improvement and modern progress are everywhere manifest.

Scarcely a day passes that does not witness some pilgrimage to this Mecca of loyal devotion to human freedom.

———

It is almost needless to state that I am still strongly attached to the place, its surroundings and associations, though for many years my home has been in another part of the State.

Fondly do I cherish the scenes of my childhood. Often do I think of the lovely groves on and around Culp's Hill ; of the mighty bowlders which there abound, upon which we often spread the picnic feast ; of the now famous Spangler's Spring, where we drank the cooling draught on those peaceful summer days. There too, our merry peals of laughter mingled with the sweet warbling of the birds. What pleasant times were ours as we went berrying along the quiet, sodded lane, that leads from the town to that now memorable hill.

From my mind can never be effaced those far off mountains to the west, whose distant horizon gave a gorgeousness to sunsets, which, when once seen, can never be forgotten. Beholding those various tinted ephemeral isles, in that sea of occidental glory, one could not help thinking of the possibilities of the grandeur in the beyond. The effect could be none other than transporting.

As I often stood in the quiet Evergreen Cemetery, when we knew naught but the smiles of Peace, gazing to the distant South Mountains, or the nearer Round Tops, or Culp's Hill, little did I dream that from those summits the engines of war wonld, in a few years, belch forth their missiles of destruction; that through those sylvan aisles would reverberate the clash of arms, the roar of musketry, and the booming of cannon, to be followed by the groans of the wounded and dying.

Little did I think that those lovely valleys

teeming with verdure and the rich harvest, would soon be strewn with the distorted and mangled bodies of American brothers; making a rich ingathering for the grim monster Death; that across that peaceful lane would charge the brave and daring "Louisiana Tigers," thirsting for their brother's blood, but soon to be hurled back filling the space over which they advanced with their shattered and dead bodies.

Such is the transition which in my girl-hood days I was made to realize.

The horrors of war are fully known only to those who have seen and heard them. It was my lot to see and hear only part, but it was sufficient.

———

To-day, many of my dear, former associates of Gettysburg are gone. The kind and sweet faces of the old fathers and mothers have passed beyond the veil. They whom I used to love and honor now sleep their last sleep beneath the sods of that memorable valley. No more will they narrate their experiences of that terrible

conflict ; nor tell how they cared for and shel-
tered the wounded ; the narrow escapes they
made from stray shots ; their property taken or
destroyed.

With pleasant recollections I bring to mind
the Young Ladies' Seminary on the corner of
High and Washington Streets. Here I received
instruction ; here in the bright and happy flush
of young womanhood, I was graduated and given
my diploma.

Within those same walls had been placed
some of the wounded and dying heroes of the
struggle ; and as we passed from room to room
we would speak in subdued tones of the solemn
scenes which imagination and report placed before
our minds as having transpired when the conflict was over.

The old College Church on Chambersburg
Street, once a battle hospital, afterwards witnessed
the ceremony that made me a happy bride.

The very streets, the homes, the sanctuaries,
even the tones of their bells, the hour's stroke
of the Court House clock, the familiar faces and

voices of the citizens at the period of which
I now write, all cling to my recollection and
are endeared to my heart, as only the memor·
ies of childhood and youth can endear.

———

My native townsmen, during that terrible
struggle, acted as patriotic and bravely as it
was possible for citizens to act, who had suddenly thrust upon them the most gigantic battle
of modern times.

They had none of the weapons or munitions
of war ; they were not drilled and were totally
unprepared for such an unthoughtof experience,
They were civilians.

Long before had many of their sons and
brothers gone to the front, and those who still
remained were as true to the Union as those
found at home in the other towns of the
North.

Upon the first rumor of the rebel invasion,
Major Robert Bell, a citizen of the place, re-
cruited a company of cavalry from the town
and surrounding country.

A company of infantry was also formed from the students and citizens of the place which was mustered into Col. Wm. Jennings' regiment of Pennsylvania Emergency Troops.

This regiment, on June 26th, was the first to encounter and exchange shots with the invaders of 1863. Though inexperienced, the stand they made, and the valor they displayed before an overwhelming force, cannot fail in placing the loyalty and bravery of her citizens in the foremost rank.

Opportunity was offered a few, who like old John Burns, went into the fray. To some like Professors Jacobs and Stower, came the occasion of explaining and pointing out to the Union officers the impregnable positions of the locality, and by this means insuring victory to our arms.

To others was given the oppottunity of concealing in their homes the brave Union boys who had been wounded in the first day's fight, who, in their retreat, had sought shelter in the house they could first reach, and there were compelled to remain, within the Confederate lines, during the remainder of the battle.

Many a Union soldier would have gone to " Libby " or " Andersonville " had it not been for the loyalty and bravery of some of the citizens in thus secreting them.

To all was presented the opportunity of caring for the wounded and dying after the battle had passed, and nobly and feebly did they administer the tender and loving acts of charity even in their own homes as well as upon the field and in the hospital.

Let those disposed to cavil and doubt the patriotism of the citizens of Gettysburg at the time of the battle forever cease, for what I have written is correct.

True it is there were a few who sympathized with the South just as in other Northern towns, but it would be unjust and unreasonable to condemn the many for the misdeeds of the few.

CHAPTER II.

INCIDENTS PRECEDING THE BATTLE.

Before entering into a description of what I saw during the battle, it may be interesting to narrate some of the preceding events that occurred.

We had often heard that the rebels were about to make a raid, but had always found it a false alarm.

An amusing incident connected with these reported raids, was the manner in which some of our older men prepared to meet the foe.

I remember one evening in particular, when quite a number of them had assembled to guard the town that night against an attack from the enemy. They were "armed to the teeth" with old, rusty guns and swords, pitchforks, shovels and pick-axes. Their falling into line, the manœuvers, the commands given and not heeded, would have done a veteran's heart good. I have often sat and listened to these well-meaning citizens laugh over the contemplation of their comical aspect.

On these occasions it was also amusing to behold the conduct of the colored people of the town. Gettysburg had a goodly number of them. They regarded the Rebels as having an especial hatred toward them, and believed that if they fell into their hands, annihilation was sure.

These folks mostly lived in the southwestern part of the town, and their flight was invariably down Breckenridge Street and Baltimore Street, and toward the woods on and around Culp's Hill.

I can see them yet; men and women with bundles as large as old-fashioned feather ticks slung across their backs, almost bearing them to the ground. Children also, carrying their bundles, and striving in vain to keep up with their seniors. The greatest consternation was depicted on all their countenances as they hurried along; crowding, and running against each other in their confusion ; children stumbling, falling, and crying. Mothers, anxious for their offspring, would stop for a moment to hurry them up, saying :

"*Fo' de Lod's sake, you chillen, cum right long quick! If dem Rebs dun kotch you, dey tear you all up;*" and similar expressions. These terrible warnings were sure to have the desired effect; for, with their eyes open wider than ever, they were not long in hastening their steps.

About three weeks before the battle, rumors were again rife of the coming of the rebel horde into our own fair and prosperous State.

This caused the greatest alarm; and our hearts often throbbed with fear and trembling. To many of us, such a visit meant destruction of home, property and perhaps life.

We were informed they had crossed the State line, then were at Chambersburg, then at Carlisle, then at or near Harrisburg, and would soon have possession of our capital.

We had often heard of their taking horses and cattle, carrying off property and destroying buildings.

A week had hardly elapsed when another alarm beset us.

" The Rebels are coming ! The Rebels are coming ! " was passed from lip to lip, and all was again consternation.

We were having our regular literary exercises on Friday afternoon, at our Seminary, when the cry reached our ears. Rushing to the door, and standing on the front portico we beheld in the direction of the Theological Seminary, a dark, dense mass, moving toward town. Our teacher, Mrs. Eyster, at once said :

" Children, run home as quickly as you can. "

It did not require repeating. I am satisfied some of the girls did not reach their homes before the Rebels were in the streets.

As for myself, I had scarcely reached the front door, when, on looking up the street, I saw some of the men on horseback. I scrambled in, slammed shut the door, and hastening to the sitting room, peeped out between the shutters.

What a horrible sight! There they were, human beings! clad almost in rags, covered with dust, riding wildly, pell-mell down the hill toward our home! shouting, yelling most unearthly, cursing, brandishing their revolvers, and firing right and left.

I was fully persuaded that the Rebels had actually come at last. What they would do with us was a fearful question to my young mind.

Soon the town was filled with infantry, and then the searching and ransacking began in earnest.

They wanted horses, clothing, anything and almost everything they could conveniently carry away.

Nor were they particular about asking. Whatever suited them they took. They did, however, make a formal demand of the town authorities, for a large supply of flour, meat, groceries, shoes, hats, and (doubtless, not least in their estimations), ten barrels of whiskey; or, in lieu of all this, five thousand dollars.

But our merchants and bankers had too often heard of their coming, and had already shipped their wealth to places of safety. Thus it was, that a few days after, the citizens of York were compelled to make up our proportion of the Rebel requisition.

I have often thought what a laughable spectacle this wing of Southern chivalry would have presented on dress parade, had they obtained and donned the variety of hats generally found upon the shelves of a village store. But they were reduced to extremity and doubtless were not particular.

Upon the report of, and just previous to this raid, the citizens had sent their horses out the Baltimore Pike, as far as the Cemetery There they were to be kept until those having the care of them were signaled that the enemy was about, when they were to hasten as fast as possible in the direction of Baltimore. Along with this party Father sent our own horse, in charge of the hired boy we then had living with us. I was very much attached to the animal, for she was gentle and very pretty. I had often ridden her.

The cavalry referred to above came so suddenly that no signal was given. They overtook the boys with the horses, captured, and brought them all back to town.

As they were passing our house my mother beckoned to the raiders, and some of them rode over to where she was standing and asked what was the matter, Mother said to them :

" You don't want the boy ! He is not our boy, he is only living with us."

One of the men replied :

" No we don't want the boy, you can have him ; we are only after the horses." About this time the boy's sister, who was standing a short distance off, screamed at the top of her voice to Mother :

" If the Rebs take our Sam, I don't know what I'll do with you folks ! " Thus holding us responsible for her brother Sam's safety even in times like that. Mother however, assured her that they were after horses and not their Sam.

After we saw that the boy was safe Mother and I began to plead for the horse. As I stood there begging and weeping, I was so shocked and insulted, I shall never forget it. One impudent and coarse Confederate said to me:

"Sissy, what are you crying about? Go in the house and mind your business."

I felt so indignant at his treatment I only wished I could have had some manner of revenge on the fellow. They left however, without giving us any satisfaction.

About one-half hour after this some of these same raiders came back, and, stopping at the kitchen door, asked Mother for something to eat. She replied:

"Yes, you ought to come back and ask for something to eat after taking a person's horse." She nevertheless gave them some food, for Mother always had a kind and noble heart even toward her enemies.

Their manner of eating was shocking in the extreme. As I stood in a doorway and saw them laughing and joking at their deeds of the day, they threw the apple butter in all directions while spreading their bread. I was heartily glad when they left, for they were a rude set.

While they were still in the kitchen, my mother pleaded earnestly for our horse, so they told her that if we would go to Colonel White, their commander, we might, perhaps, get the horse back.

Father went with them; but when he got before Colonel White, he was informed by that officer that he understood father was " A black Abolitionist; so black, that he was turning black;" also, that he understood that he had two sons in the Union Army, whom he supposed had taken as much from the South as they were now taking from him. So my father returned without the horse.

This information given to the Rebels, we afterwards learned, was the act of Sam's sister, referred to above. I am afraid her sympathies were not as much for the Union as they should have been. She certainly manifested a very unkind disposition toward our family, who had been doing all we could for her brother. It would surprise a great many to learn who this person was, but as no detraction is intended, I will dismiss the subject at once.

We frequently saw the Rebels riding our horse up and down the street, until at last she became so lame she could hardly get along. That was the last we saw of her, and I felt that I had been robbed of a dear friend.

While the infantry were moving about the town in squads searching for booty, and while we were all standing at the front door look-ing at their movements and wondering what they would do next, I remember that my mother, not noticing any in the immediate vicinity, spoke to a neighbor on the opposite side of the street saying :

" What a filthy, dirty looking set ! One cannot tell them from the street." Father said: " You had better be careful ; there is one of them at the curb-stone right in front of us tying his shoe." Mother exclaimed ;

" Oh   my !   I   didn't   see   him ! "

They   were   actually   so   much   the   color   of
the   street,   that   it   was   no   wonder   we   failed   to
notice   this   one.

That   evening   when   these   raiders   were   leaving,   they   ran   all   the   cars   that   were   about,   out
to   the   railroad   bridge   east   of   the   town,   set
the   bridge   and   cars   on   fire   and   destroyed   the
track.   We   were   informed   that   they   had   gone
to   York,   a   thriving   town   about   twenty-five
miles   to   the   northeast.

————

A   little   before   noon   on   Tuesday,   June   30th,
a   great   number   of   Union   cavalry   began   to   arrive
in   the   town.   They   passed   northwardly   along
Washington   Street,   turned   toward   the   west   on
reaching   Chambersburg   Street,   and   passed   out
in   the   direction   of   the   Theological   Seminary.

It   was   to   me   a   novel   and   grand   sight.
I   had   never   seen   so   many   soldiers   at   one
time.   They   were   Union   soldiers   and   that   was
enough   for   me,   for   I   then   knew   we   had   protection,   and   I   felt   they   were   our   dearest   friends,

I afterwards learned that these men were Buford's cavalry, numbering about six thousand men.

A crowd of " us girls " were standing on the corner of Washington and High Streets as these soldiers passed by. Desiring to encourage them, who, as we were told, would before long be in battle, my sister started to sing the old war song " Our Union Forever." As some of us did not know the whole of the piece we kept repeating the chorus.

Thus we sought to cheer our brave men; and we felt amply repaid when we saw that our efforts were appreciated. Their countenances brightened and we received their thanks and cheers.

After the battle some of these soldiers told us that the singing was very good, but that they would have liked to have heard more than the chorus.

The movements of this day in addition to what we beheld a few days previous, told plainly that some great military event was coming pretty close to us. The town was all astir and every one was anxious.

Thus in the midst of great excitement and solicitude the day passed. As we lay down for the night, little did we think what the morrow would bring forth.

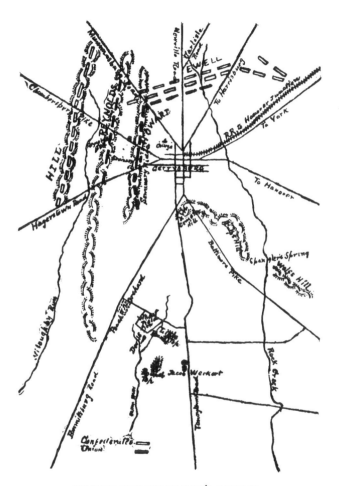

MAP OF THE FIRST DAY'S BATTLE.

CHAPTER III.

We awoke early. It was impossible to become drowsy with the events of the previous day uppermost in our minds. We were prompt enough at breakfast that morning.

As more soldiers were expected, and in order to show how welcome they would be, my sister and I had, on the previous evening, prepared a tableful of boquets which we intended to hand or throw to them as they passed our house.

We had no sooner finished our breakfast when it was announced that troops were coming. We hastened up what we called the side street, (Breckenridge,) and on reaching Washington Street, again saw some of our army passing.

First came a long line of cavalry, then wagon after wagon passed by for quite awhile. Again we sang patriotic songs as they moved along. Some of these wagons were filled with stretchers and other articles; in others we noticed soldiers reclining, who were doubtless in some way disabled.

It was between nine and ten o'clock when we first noticed firing in the direction of Seminary Ridge. At first the sound was faint, then it grew louder. Soon the booming of cannon was heard, then great clouds of smoke were seen rising beyond the ridge. The sound became louder and louder, and was now incessant. The troops passing us moved faster, the men had now become excited and urged on their horses. The battle was waging. This was my first terrible experience.

I remember hearing some of the soldiers remarking that there was no telling how soon some of them would be brought back in those ambulances, or carried on the stretchers. I hardly knew what it meant, but I learned afterward, even before the day had passed.

It was almost noon when the last of the train had passed, and I began to think of dinner and the folks at home.

I hurried back, and the first thing that
met my gaze as I passed the parlor was the
table full of flowers. The soldiers had passed
and we had not given them the boquets.
They did not come by our house and in our
haste to see them, we had forgotten all about
the intended welcome.

Entering the dining-room I found dinner
waiting, but I was too excited to eat, and so,
soon finished my meal. After I had eaten
what that day I called dinner, our neighbor,
Mrs. Schriver, called at the house and said she
would leave the town and go to her father's
(Jacob Weikert), who lived on the Taneytown
road at the eastern slope of the Round Top.

Mr. Schriver, her husband, was then serving in the Union army, so that under all the
circumstances at this time surrounding her, Mrs.
Schriver did not feel safe in the house.

As the battle had commenced and was still
progressing at the west of the town, and was
not very far off, she thought it safer for her-

self and two children to go to her parents, who lived about three miles to the south. She requested that I be permitted to accompany her, and as it was regarded a safer place for me than to remain in town, my parents readily consented that I should go.

The only preparation I made for the departure, was to carry my best clothes down to the cellar, so that they might be safe when I returned; never thinking of taking any along, nor how long I would stay.

———

About one o'clock we started on foot; the battle still going on. We proceeded out Baltimore Street and entered the Evergreen Cemetery. This was our easiest and most direct route, as it would bring us to the Taneytown road a little further on.

As we were passing along the Cemetery hill, our men were already planting cannon.

They told us to hurry as fast as possible; that we were in great danger of being shot

FLEEING FROM DANGER.

by the Rebels, whom they expected would shell toward us at any moment. We fairly ran to get out of this new danger.

As I looked toward the Seminary Ridge I could see and hear the confusion of the battle. Troops moving hither and thither; the smoke of the conflict arising from the fields ; shells bursting in the air, together with the din, rising and falling in mighty undulations. These things, beheld for the first time, filled my soul with the greatest apprehensions.

We soon reached the Taneytown road, and while traveling along, were overtaken by an ambulance wagon in which was the body of a dead soldier. Some of the men told us that it was the body of General Reynolds, and that he had been killed during the forenoon in the battle.

We continued on our way, and had gotten to a little one and a half story house, stand-ing on the west side of the road, when, on account of the muddy condition of the road, we were compelled to stop. This place on the following day became General Meade's head-quarters.

While we were standing at the gate, not knowing what to do or where to go, a soldier came out and kindly told us he would try to get some way to help us further on, as it was very dangerous to remain there.

It began to look as though we were getting into new dangers at every step, instead of getting away from them.

We went into the house and after waiting a short time, this same soldier came to us saying :

" Now I have a chance for you. There is a wagon coming down the road and I will try to get them to make room for you."

The wagon was already quite full, but the soldier insisted and prevailed. We fully appreciated his kindness, and as he helped us on the wagon we thanked him very much.

But what a ride ! I shall never forget it. The mud was almost up to the hubs of the wheels, and underneath the mud were rocks.

The wagon had no springs, and as the driver was anxious to put the greatest distance between himself and the battle in the least time possible, the jolting and bumping were brought out to perfection.

At last we reached Mr. Weikert's and were gladly welcomed to their home.

It was not long after our arrival, until Union artillery came hurrying by. It was indeed a thrilling sight. How the men impelled their horses! How the officers urged the men as they all flew past toward the sound of the battle! Now the road is getting all cut up; they take to the fields, and all is an anxious, eager hurry! Shouting, lashing the horses, cheering the men, they all rush madly on.

Suddenly we behold an explosion; it is that of a caisson. We see a man thrown high in the air and come down in a wheat field close by. He is picked up and carried into the house. As they pass by I see his eyes are blown out and his whole person seems to be one black mass. The first words I hear him say is:

"Oh dear! I forgot to read my Bible to-day! What will my poor wife and children say?"

I saw the soldiers carry him up stairs; they laid him upon a bed and wrapped him in cotton. How I pitied that poor man! How terribly the scenes of war were being irresistibly portrayed before my vision.

After the artillery had passed, infantry began coming. I soon saw that these men were very thirsty and would go to the spring which is on the north side of the house.

I was not long in learning what I could do. Obtaining a bucket, I hastened to the spring, and there, with others, carried water to the moving column until the spring was empty. We then went to the pump standing on the south side of the house, and supplied water from it. Thus we continued giving water to our tired soldiers until night came on, when we sought rest indoors.

It was toward the close of the afternoon of this day that some of the wounded from the field of battle began to arrive where I was staying. They reported hard fighting, many wounded and killed, and were afraid our troops would be defeated and perhaps routed.

The first wounded soldier whom I met had his thumb tied up. This I thought was dreadful, and told him so.

" Oh," said he, " this is nothing; you'll see worse than this before long."

'Oh! I hope not," I innocently replied.

Soon two officers carrying their arms in slings made their appearance, and I more fully began to realize that something terrible had taken place.

Now the wounded began to come in greater numbers. Some limping, some with their heads and arms in bandages, some crawling, others carried on stretchers or brought in ambulances. Suffering, cast down and dejected, it was a truly pitiable gathering. Before night the barn was filled with the shattered and dying heroes of this day's struggle.

That evening Beckie Weikert, the daughter at home, and I went out to the barn to see what was transpiring there. Nothing before in my experience had ever paralleled the sight we then and there beheld. There were the groaning and crying, the struggling and dying, crowded side by side, while attendants sought to aid and relieve them as best they could.

We were so overcome by the sad and awful spectacle that we hastened back to the house weeping bitterly.

As we entered the basement or cellar-kitchen of the house, we found many nurses making beef tea for the wounded. Seeing that we were crying they inquired as to the cause. We told them where we had been and what we had seen. They no doubt appreciated our feelings for they at once endeavored to cheer us by telling funny stories, and ridiculing our tears. They soon dispelled our terror and caused us to laugh so much that many times when we should have been sober minded we were not; the reaction having been too sudden for our overstrung nerves.

I remember that at this time a chaplain who was present in the kitchen stepped up to me while I was attending to some duty and said:

"Little girl, do all you can for the poor soldiers and the Lord will reward you."

I looked up in his face and laughed, but at once felt ashamed of my conduct and begged his pardon. After telling him what Beckie and I had seen, how the nurses had derided us for crying and that I now laughed when I should not, being unable to help myself, he remarked:

"Well it is much better for you and the soldiers to be in a cheerful mood."

The first day had passed, and with the rest of the family, I retired, surrounded with strange and appalling events, and many new visions passing rapidly through my mind.

CHAPTER IV.

The day dawned bright and clear; the hot rays of the July sun soon fell upon the landscape.

As quickly as possible I hurried out of the house, and saw more troops hurrying toward town.

About ten o'clock many pieces of artillery and large ammunition trains came up, filling the open space to the east of us. Regiment after regiment continued to press forward.

I soon engaged in the occupation of the previous day; that of carrying water to the soldiers as they passed.

How often my thoughts were anxiously fixed on my dear ones at home as the troops hurried along toward town. Were they well? Were they alive? Did I still have a home? These, with many other silent inquiries, sprang to my mind without any hope of an answer.

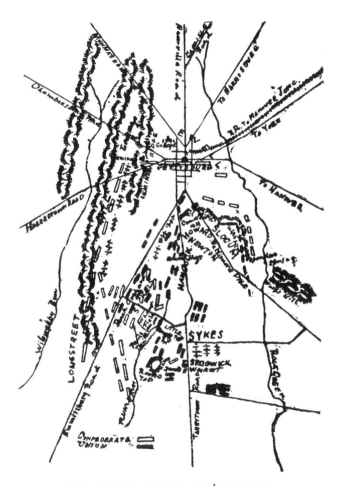

MAP OF THE SECOND DAY'S BATTLE.

It was impossible in the present state of affairs to expect any tidings from them.

During the early part of the forenoon my attention was called to numerous rough boxes which had been placed along the road just outside the garden fence. Ominous and dismal as was the sight presented, it nevertheless did not prevent some of the soldiers from passing jocular expressions. One of the men near by, being addressed with the remark that there was no telling how soon he would be put in one of them, replied :

" I will consider myself very lucky if I *get* one."

This forenoon another incident occurred which I shall ever remember. While the infantry were passing, I noticed a poor, worn-out soldier crawling along on his hands and knees. An officer yelled at him, with cursing, to get up and march. The poor fellow said he could not, whereupon the officer, raising his sword, struck him down three or four times. The officer passed on, little caring what he had done. Some of his comrades at once picked up the prostrate form and carried the unfortunate man into the house. After several hours of hard work the sufferer was brought back to consciousness. He seemed quite a young man, and was suffering from sunstroke received on the forced march. As they were carrying him in, some of the men who had witnessed this act of brutality remarked:

"We will mark that officer for this."

It is a pretty well established fact that many a brutal officer fell in battle, from being shot other than by the enemy.

Shortly after this occurrence, and while still supplying water to the passing troops, from the pump, three officers on horseback came riding up to the gate. The centre one kindly requested me to give him a drink. I asked him to please excuse the tin cup I then held in my hand. He replied:

"Certainly; that is all right."

After he had drunk he thanked me very pleasantly. The other two officers did not wish any.

As they were about turning away, the soldiers around gave three cheers for General Meade. The one to whom I had given the drink turned his horse about, made me a nice bow, and then saluted the soldiers. They then rode rapidly away. I asked a soldier:

"Who did you say that officer was?" He replied:

"General Meade."

Some time after this several field officers came into the house and asked permission to go on the roof in order to make observations, As I was not particularly engaged at the time, and could be most readily spared, I was told to show them the way up. They opened a trap door and looked through their field-glasses at the grand panorama spread out below.

By and by they asked me if I would like to look. Having expressed my desire to do so they gave me the glasses. The sight I then beheld was wonderful and sublime.

The country for miles around seemed to

be filled with troops; artillery moving here and there as fast as they could go; long lines of infantry forming into position; officers on horseback galloping hither and thither! It was a grand and awful spectacle, and impressed me as being some great review.

During the whole of this afternoon Mrs. Weikert and her daughters were busy baking bread for the soldiers. As soon as one ovenful was baked it was replenished with new, and the freshly baked loaves at once cut up and distributed. How eagerly and gratefully the tired-out men received this food! They stated that they had not tasted such sweet bread for a long time. Perhaps it was because they were eating it once more on loyal soil.

It was shortly before noon that I observed soldiers lying on the ground just back of the house, dead. They had fallen just where they had been standing when shot. I was told that they had been picked off by Rebel sharpshooters, who were up in Big Round Top.

Toward the middle of the afternoon heavy cannonading began on the two Round Tops just back of the house. This was so terrible and severe that it was with great difficulty we could hear ourselves speak. It began very unexpectedly; so much so, that we were all terror-stricken, and hardly knew what to do.

Some of the soldiers suggested that we had better go to a farm house about one-half a mile across the fields to the east; and acting on their advice we ran thither as fast as we could.

On our way over, my attention was suddenly attracted, in the direction of the town, to what seemed a sheet of lightning. This bright light remained in the sky quite awhile. The first thought that flashed upon my mind was, perhaps it is Gettysburg burning; and so expressed my fear to some of the soldiers we were then passing. One of the men more bent on mischief than on sympathy, said:

" Yes, that is Gettysburg and all the people in it."

This made me cry, for I thought at once of the dear ones at home.

When we reached the farm-house some of the soldiers who were about the place, seeing me in tears, were touched with compassion, and asked the cause. I told him what had been said to me, and that my parents and sister were in the town. They assured me that in war the rule was, always to allow helpless and innocent citizens to get out of a place, and never to destroy them. I then felt comforted, and they further told me that the light I saw was some signal.

Here we were permitted to remain but a few minutes, for hardly had we arrived at our supposed place of refuge, when we were told to hurry back to where we came from ; that we were in a great deal more danger, from the fact that the shells would fall just about this place, whereas at the house near Round Top the shells would pass over us. So there was no alternative but to retrace our steps about as fast as we came,

During our flight over to the farm-house, and when about half way, Mrs. Weikert happened to think of some highly prized article of dress, that in our sudden flight she had never thought of. Nothing would do but that her husband would have to go back to the house and get it. Thus in the midst of the confusion of battle, Mr. Weikert started back. Just as we were reaching our starting point, we met him coming out with the treasure; a brand new quilted petticoat; and we all went panting into the house.

During the whole of this wild goose chase the cannonading had become terrible! Occasionally a shell would come flying over Round Top and explode high in the air over head Just before leaving so hurriedly, a baking had been put in the old-fashioned oven; when we came back we expected to find it all burned, but fortunately the soldiers had taken it out in good time. They doubtless had their eye on it as well as on the enemy.

The cannonading, which all the time appeared

to be getting more and more severe, lasted until the close of day.

It seemed as though the heavens were send-ing forth peal upon peal of terrible thunder, directly over our heads; while at the same time, the very earth beneath our feet trembled. The cannonading at Gettysburg, has already gone down into history as terrible.

Those who are familiar with this battle now know what havoc and destruction were accom-plished on this afternoon, on the west side of the Round Tops, at Devil's Den, Sherby's Peach Orchard and the Wheat-field.

During the heavy firing of which I have just spoken, and while Mr. Weikert was in the house searching for the treasure heretofore mentioned, he heard something heavy, fall inside the enclosed stairway. Suddenly the door was burst open, when out rolled the poor soldier who had been wrapped in cotton. He had become terrified at the heavy peals of artillery, and springing from his bed in his blindness, groped around, trying to find the stairs. He was again carried up and after that someone remained with him. This occurrence delayed Mr. Weikert in returning to us across the fields, and hence it was that we met him just leaving the house on our return.

Between four and five o'clock in the afternoon, I heard some of the soldiers about the house saying:

"The Rebels are on this side of Round Top, coming across the fields toward the house, and there will be danger if they get on the Taneytown road."

Just then some one said that the Pennsylvania Reserves were on the way, and having a brother in the First Regiment of the Reserves I was anxious to see whether he would be along.

As I went out to the south side of the house I looked in the direction of Round Top, and there saw the Rebels moving rapidly in our direction.

Suddenly I heard the sound of fife and drum coming from the other side of the barn.

Then some of our soldiers shouted:

"There come the Pennsylvania Reserves!"
And sure enough there they were, coming on
a double-quick between the barn and Round
Top, firing as they ran.

The Confederates faced toward them, fired,
halted, and then began to retreat. I saw
them falling as they were climbing over a
stone wall and as they were shot in the open
space. The fighting lasted but a short time,
when the Confederates were driven back in the
direction of Little Round Top. I think they
passed between the Round Tops.

On this evening the number of wounded
brought to the place was indeed appalling.
They were laid in different parts of the house.
The orchard and space around the buildings
were covered with the shattered and dying,
and the barn became more and more crowded.
The scene had become terrible beyond description.

That night, in the house, I made myself
useful in doing whatever I could to assist the

CHARGE OF THE PENNSYLVANIA RESERVES.

surgeons and nurses. Cooking and making beef tea seemed to be going on all the time. It was an animated and busy scene. Some were cutting bread and spreading it, while I was kept busy carrying the pieces to the soldiers.

One soldier, sitting near the doorway that led into a little room in the southeast corner of the basement, beckoned me to him. He was holding a lighted candle in his hand, and was watching over a wounded soldier who was lying upon the floor. He asked me if I would get him a piece of bread, saying he was very hungry. I said certainly, ran away and soon returned. I gave him the bread and he seemed very thankfnl. He then asked me if I would hold the light and stay with the wounded man until he came back. I said I would gladly do so, and that I wanted to do something for the poor soldiers if I only knew what.

I then took the candle and sat down beside the wounded man. I talked to him and asked if he was injured badly. He answered :

"Yes, pretty badly."

I then asked him if he suffered much, to which he replied :

"Yes, I do now, but I hope in the morning I will be better."

I told him if there was anything I could do for him I would be so glad to do it, if he would only tell me what. The poor man looked so earnestly into my face, saying :

"Will you promise me to come back in the morning to see me."

I replied : "Yes, indeed." And he seemed so satisfied, and faintly smiled.

The man who had been watching him now returned, and thanked me for my kindness. I gave him the light and arose to leave.

The poor wounded soldier's eyes followed me, and the last words he said to me were :

"Now don't forget your promise." I replied :

"No indeed," and expressing the hope

that he would be better in the morning, bade him good night.

———

CHAPTER V.

The sun was high in the heavens when I awoke the next day.

The first thought that came into my mind, was my promise of the night before.

I hastened down to the little basement room, and as I entered, the soldier lay there— dead. His faithful attendant was still at his side.

I had kept my promise, but he was not there to greet me. I hope he greeted nearer and dearer faces than that of the unknown little girl on the battle-field of Gettysburg.

As I stood there gazing in sadness at the prostrate form, the attendant looked up to me and asked: "Do you know who this is?" I replied: "No sir." He said: "This is the body of General Weed; a New York man."

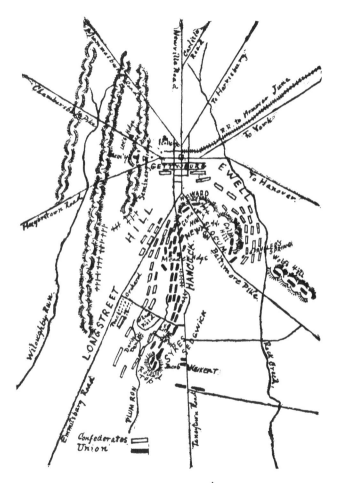

MAP OF THE THIRD DAY'S BATTLE.

As concerning many other incidents of the late war, so with the death of this brave general, I find an erroneous judgment has been formed ; some claiming that he was instantly killed on Little Round Top, during the fight of the second day.

That General Weed was mortally wounded on Little Round Top while assisting at Hazlett's battery on account of the scarcity of gunners, is well established. That Lieutenant Hazlett was instantly killed, while bending over the prostrate form of his commander to catch his dying message, is also undisputed ; but that General Weed *died* on Little Round Top is a mistake.

What is more likely than, that after being severely wounded, he should be taken down the eastern slope of the hill, away from the conflict, reaching the Taneytown road at its base ? What more probable than, on reaching that road that they should carry his body away from th field by going toward the south ? Why would they *not* carry him into Mr. Weikert's house when that was the first place they reached, that was used as a battle hospital ?

Doubtless General Weed was carried from the field as dead, but the place and circum - stances of his death, are given in the preceding lines.

I could never forget that name, and always remembered it by reason of the similarity of sound with that of General Meade, whom I had also seen that same day, when I handed him a drink.

———

But to return to the passing events.

Tired-out with the strain and exciting scenes of the previous day, I was still sound asleep when the family had finished breakfast ; so that when I got down stairs all traces of the morning meal had been cleared away.

While in conversation with the soldier beside the body of General Weed, as above related, I was told by some one, that the carriages were in waiting out at the barn, to take us off to a place of safety.

Already there was occasional musketry and cannonading in the direction of Gettysburg, and we expected greater danger than at any time before.

Some of the soldiers told us that they had planted cannon on two sides of the house, and that if the Rebels attempted to reach the Taneytown road, as they had the day before, there would likely be hard fighting right around the house ; and that if we remained, we would be in the midst of flying bullets and shell. Under these circumstances we made all possible haste to depart.

When we reached the carriages, and were about to get in, a shell came screaming through the air directly overhead. I was so frightened that I gave a shriek and sprang into the barn. Even with their suffering, the poor fellows could not help laughing at my terror and sudden appearance. One of them near me said :

" My child, if that had hit you, you would not have had time to jump." Pretty sound logic. Just after I jumped into the barn, I noticed that the shell had struck in the adjoining field, without exploding.

We then got into the carriages as quickly as possible, and started for a place of safety.

A short distance below the barn we came to quite a number of troops, who were drawn up in line as if held in reserve. Upon inquiry, we were informed that they belonged to the Sixth Corps.

After proceding a mile or so down the Taneytown road, we turned to the left and crossed over to the Baltimore Pike, near the Two Taverns.

Between the Taneytown road and the Baltimore pike, we passed through a strip of woods, where, some of the soldiers told us, there had been a cavalry fight just an hour previous. Here I first saw Rebel prisoners ; there was a whole field filled with them. Their appearance was very rough, and they seemed completely tired out.

While we were talking with our soldiers, I noticed one eating a " hard tack ". I, having had nothing to eat as yet that day, and being quite hungry, must have looked very wistfully at him, for he reached into his haver-sack and presented me with one of those army delicacies. I accepted it with thanks, and nothing that I can recall was ever more relished, or tasted sweeter, than that Union soldier's biscuit, eaten on July 3, 1863.

We finally arrived at a farm house beyond the pike, and found the place full of people who had also fled from their homes, to get beyond the dangers of the battle.

Toward the close of the afternoon it was noticed that the roar of the battle was sub-siding, and after all had become quiet we started back for Mr. Weikert's home. As we drove along in the cool of the evening, we noticed that everywhere confusion prevailed. Fences were thrown down near and far; knap-sacks, blankets and many other articles, lay scattered here and there. The whole country seemed filled with desolation.

Upon reaching the place I fairly shrank

back   aghast   at   the   awful   sight   presented. The approaches were crowded with wounded, dying and dead.   The   air   was   filled   with   moanings, and groanings.   As we passed on toward the house, we were compelled to pick our steps in order   that   we   might   not   tread   on   the   prostrate   bodies.

When we entered the house we found it also completely filled with the wounded. We hardly knew   what   to   do   or   where   to   go.   They, however,   removed   most   of   the   wounded,   and thus after a while made room for the family.

As   soon   as   possible, we   endeavored   to make ourselves useful by rendering assistance in this heartrending state of affairs.   I remember that Mrs. Weikert went through the house, and after   searching   awhile,   brought   all   the   muslin and linen she could spare.   This we tore into bandages   and   gave   them   to   the   surgeons, to bind up the poor soldier's wounds.

By this time, amputating benches had been placed about the house.   I must have become inured to seeing the   terrors of battle, else I could hardly have gazed upon the scenes now presented. I was looking out one of the windows facing the front yard. Near the basement door, and directly underneath the window I was at, stood one of these benches. I saw them lifting the poor men upon it, then the surgeons sawing and cutting off arms and legs, then again probing and picking bullets from the flesh.

Some of the soldiers fairly begged to be taken next, so great was their suffering, and so anxious were they to obtain relief.

I saw the surgeons hastily put a cattle horn over the mouths of the wounded ones, after they were placed upon the bench. At first I did not understand the meaning of this but upon inquiry, soon learned that that was their mode of administering chloroform, in order to produce unconsciousness. But the effect in some instances was not produced ; for I saw the wounded throwing themselves wildly about, and shrieking with pain while the operation was going on.

To the south of the house, and just out-side of the yard, I noticed a pile of limbs higher than the fence. It was a ghastly sight! Gazing upon these, too often the trophies of the amputating bench, I could have no other feeling, than that the whole scene was one of cruel butchery.

But I do not desire to dwell upon such pictures any longer, for they are the most horrible that the battle presented to my mind.

Twilight had now fallen ; another day had closed ; with the soldiers saying, that they be-lieved this day the Rebels were whipped, but at an awful sacrifice.

CHAPTER VI.

AFTER THE BATTLE.

It was the Fourth of July, and never has the cheering on that anniversary been more hearty and welcome than it was in 1863.

On the summits, in the valleys, everywhere we heard the soldiers hurrahing for the victory that had been won. The troops on our right, at Culp's Hill, caught up the joyous sound as it came rolling on from the Round Tops on our left, and soon the whole line of blue, rejoiced in the results achieved. Many a dying hero's last breath, carried a thanksgiving and praise to Him, who had watched over, and directed the thoughts and movements of the last three days. Most befitting was it, that on the fourth of July, an overruling and all-wise Providence should again declare this people, free and independent of the tyranny upheld by an enemy. Again had our natal day been recognized and honored by vouchsafing a new and purified existence to our nation, whose very life had been trembling on the brink of destruction, during this terrible ordeal.

We were all glad that the storm had passed, and that victory was perched upon our banners.

But oh! the ..orror and desolation that remained. The general destruction, the suffering, the dead, the homes that nevermore would be cheered, the heart-broken widows, the innocent and helpless orphans! Only those who have seen these things, can ever realize what they mean.

May the heart of this fair land be forever inclined unto wisdom, so that we may never fall into the folly of another war, and be compelled to pay the fearful penalty that is sure to follow.

For a number of days after the battle, amputating, nursing and cooking continued on the premises, after which the wounded were removed to the different corps' hospitals. During this time many a brave and noble spirit went from its tenement, and passed to the great beyond. This is what it meant, when they silently carried out a closed rough box, placed it upon a wagon and drove away.

———

A day or so after the battle, a soldier approached me and spoke as though he were acquainted. His face seemed familiar, yet I could not just then remember of ever having met him ; whereupon he asked me if I did not recollect the soldier who got me on the wagon during the first day's fight. I then recognized him, and was very glad to greet him once again, and to express my thanks for his kindness. Before leaving, he presented me with a relic, it being a button which he cut from a Confederate's coat, to which was attached a piece of the gray cloth. I have it yet, and is one of my most highly prized relics of those thrilling days.

———

During the battle I met a captain of artillery, who occasionally came to Mr. Weikert's

house.   He   was   a   kind, pleasant and intelli-
gent   man,   whose   very   countenance   told   me
that he possessed a soul of honor and sympathy, and which at once inspired a confidence.
As soon as he learned that my residence was
in Gettysburg, and knew how concerned I was
about my home folks, he kindly told me that
he would do his very best to visit them, and
acquaint them of my safety.   I then told him
how he could find the place, by noticing a
row of Linden trees standing in front of a
double brick house, and by other indications.

He   came   to   the   place   every   day, saying
he   had   been   to   see   my   mother, thus trying
to cheer me.   I always detected that he had
not been there, for when I asked him to tell
me the number of trees standing in front of
the house, or give me some other assurance,
he invariably failed.   Then he would encourage
me by saying he would go there just as soon
as he could get into the town.

On   the   evening   of   the   4th, this captain
came   into   the   basement   kitchen,   where,   in

company with a number of surgeons and nurses, I was sitting at a table, eating supper. He hurried to me and said :

" Now *this* time I was at your mother's."

I again began my usual inquiries, how many trees in front of the house, etc., to which he replied :

" I don't care how many trees there are, but to convince you, your mother told me all about your horse being stolen, and that Jennie Wade had been killed while baking bread for her sick sister."

" I soon learned from the conversation, that he had been to my home, and had seen and conversed with my parents and sister. I felt very grateful to him for his kindness, as it was a great comfort to know that no harm had befallen them, and that he had conveyed to them the happy intelligence of my safety.

Should any of those who sat around the table that evening be still living, they will doubtless recall the conversation between that little girl and the artillery captain. I can

still see how they laughed at and twitted the
captain on account of the searching questions
I put to him.

I saw this friend a few times afterwards,
then he was gone, I hope he passed safely
through the war, is still living, and will remember the incident I have just narrated.

———

On the following day, July 5th, I accompanied Beckie Weikert and her friend, Lieuten
ant George Kitzmiller of the First Pennsylvania
Reserves, and whom she afterwards married, on
a trip to Little Round Top.

As the Lieutenant's company was raised
from our town, and as one of my brothers
was a member of the company, I eagerly inquired whether he also had been in this battle. He informed me that my brother had
been taken very sick on the Peninsula, and
was still in the hospital at Washington. It
was a great satisfaction to know he was still
living, though I was very sorry to hear of
his sickness.

While we were climbing up Little Round Top we met one of the Pennsylvania " Buck Tails", who walked with us and pointed out the different places where the bodies lay among the rocks.

By this time the Union dead had been principally carried off the field, and those that remained were Confederates.

As we stood upon those mighty bowlders, and looked down into the chasms between, we beheld the dead lying there just as they had fallen during the struggle. From the summit of Little Round Top, surrounded by the wrecks of battle, we gazed upon the valley of death beneath. The view there spread out before us was terrible to contemplate! It was an awful spectacle! Dead soldiers, bloated horses, shattered cannon and caissons, thousands of small arms. In fact everything belonging to army equipments, was there in one confused and indescribable mass.

Here again, I had the advantage of a field glass, for there were also some officers

present who kindly gave me an opportunity of
thus viewing the field.

———

On account of the confusion everywhere
abounding, and the impassable condition of the
roads, it was thought best for me to remain
at Mr. Weikert's for several days after the
battle, and especially since my folks knew I
was safe.

Sometime during the forenoon of Tuesday,
the 7th, in company with Mrs. Schriver and
her two children, I started off on foot to reach
my home.

As it was impossible to travel the roads,
on account of the mud, we took to the fields.
While passing along, the stench arising from
the fields of carnage was most sickening. Dead
horses, swollen to almost twice their natural
size, lay in all directions, stains of blood frequently met our gaze, and all kinds of army
accoutrements covered the ground. Fences had
disappeared, some buildings were gone, others
ruined. The whole landscape had been changed,

and I felt as though we were in a strange and blighted land. Our killed and wounded had by this time been nearly all carried from the field. With such surroundings I made my journey homeward, after the battle.

We finally reached and passed through the Evergreen Cemetery, and beheld the broken monuments and confusion that reigned throughout that heretofore peaceful and silent city of the dead.

We passed out through the now shattered archway of the lodge, stood awhile to look at the barricade and battery on the Baltimore pike, and the wrecks and confusion extending over to Culp's Hill. After a few minutes more walk we reached our homes.

I hastened into the house. Everything seemed to be in confusion, and my home did not look exactly as it did when I left. Large bundles had been prepared, and were lying around in different parts of the room I had entered. They had expected to be compelled to leave the town suddenly. I soon found my mother and the rest. At first glance even my mother did not recognize me, so dilapidated was my general appearance. The only clothes I had along had by this time become covered with mud, the greater part of which was gathered the day on which we left home.

They had not been thinking just then of my return. My sudden appearance, and the sad plight I was in, were the cause of their not recognizing me at once. There was no girl at Mr. Weikert's of my size, hence it was imposisble to furnish me with other clothes, even had they had the time to think of such a thing.

As soon as I spoke my mother ran to me, and clasping me in her arms, said :

" Why, my dear child, is that you? How glad I am to have you home again without any harm having befallen you ! "

I was soon told that my clothes were still down in the cellar on the wood pile, just where I had put them, and that I should go at once and make myself presentable.

For many days, I related to the ones at home, and to others who had heard of my adventures, the scenes and trials through which I had passed during my absence. Those at home, also, had many interesting and thrilling experiences to narrate, to the recital of which the next chapter will be principally devoted.

CHAPTER VII.

HOME.

Sometime after the battle had commenced, my father went down street, he having heard that the wounded were being brought to the warehouses located in the Northern part of the town.

Desiring to assist all he could, he remained there, working for the poor sufferers until pretty late in the afternoon.

Some of the wounded had been piteously calling and begging for liquor in order to deaden the pain which racked their bodies. Father, knowing that the dealers had removed that article out of town, said he would go to some private parties, and try to obtain it. His search however was fruitless, as no one seemed to have any.

It was while thus moving around on this errand, that he noticed our men were fast retreating through the streets, and hurrying in the direction of the Cemetery.

Knowing that his family were alone, he concluded it was best to hasten to them.

On his way home, he stopped for a few minutes at a place just a square west of our house, on some business he wished to attend to. When he came out, there was no sign of Union soldiers.

As he was approaching his home, he noticed a Rebel crossing the street, a short distance beyond. He looked at my Father who was entirely alone, stopped, and halloed :

" What are you doing with that gun in your hand ?·" Father, who was in his shirt sleeves, threw up his arms and said :

" I have no gun ! " Whereupon the Confederate deliberately took aim and fired.

As soon as Father saw him taking aim, he threw himself down, and had no sooner done so, when he heard the " zip " of the bullet. In the parlance of to-day, that would be styled " a close call."

The murderous Rebel passed on ; no doubt

concluding that he made one Yankee the less.

As soon as he had passed down Baltimore Street, Father got up, and had almost reached the house, when he was spied and overtaken by a squad of five Confederates coming down an alley, and who greeted him by saying:

"Old man, why ain't you in your house?"

He replied that he was getting there just as fast as he could. They however commanded:

"Fall in!" He certainly did so, and accompanied them until he reached the front porch, when he stepped up and said:

"Now boys, I am home, and I am going to stay here."

They did not insist on taking him along, but demanded to search the house for Union soldiers; to which Father replied:

"Boys you may take my word for it; there are no Union soldiers in the house." They believed him, and passed on.

While he was still sitting on the porch, several

other squads of Rebels passed. These also wanted to search the house ; some even threatening to break the door open. They were however persuaded to desist, on being told by Father, that it was against the rules of war to break into private houses ; that he knew the family were very much frightened : and that he would give his word for it, that there were no Union soldiers in the house. One of the Confederates then exclaimed:

"Boys, I take that gentleman's word."

"By the way, what are your proclivities ? " asked one of the men. Father replied:

"I am an unconditional Union man ; and to back it up, I am a whole-souled one."

One of the group then replied:

"Well, we like you all the better for that ; for we hate the milk and water Unionists."

Before leaving, they told Father, that he had better get into the house, that *they* would not shoot him, but that he was in danger of being shot by his own men, since the Union sharp-shooters out by the Cemetery, were already sending their bullets pretty fast in that direction.

Finding the front, as well as all the other doors securely locked, he was obliged to enter the house by the back cellar door.

After he got in, imagine his surprise and consternation, after what he had just been telling, to find no less than five Union soldiers in the house. They were all sick and disabled ; two of them were captains, and were very badly wounded.

Mother nursed them and dressed their wounds during all the time of the battle. Often would they express their gratitude for her kindness and attention.

As a rule the folks stayed in the cellar during the day, as that was considered the safest place, and it was only at night after the firing had ceased, that they ventured up into the house. Very little undisturbed sleep did they enjoy during those nights.

We never heard from the five wounded men who had been nursed in the house,

except that after a period of twenty-five years,
one of them returned and made himself known.

It was on the first of July, 1888, exactly
twenty-five years from the time he retreated into our
house, that the same soldier, with his little
son, stopped at the front door, and asked if
the family was still living there that had been
during the battle. He was informed that the
only one left of those who nursed him was
my father, now in his eighty third year. We
told him that the kind mother who dressed
his wounds and waited on him was no more
on earth, and that my sister, who also assisted,
had preceded her some years.

He felt quite disappointed at not meeting
his kind benefactresses, but was still glad to
meet and talk with my father, of the thrilling
times they had spent together in different parts
of the house.

He related to us his experiences, among
which he told, how, during one night the
Rebels came up into the house from the

cellar. Hearing them come, he crawled under a settee that was standing in the hall. This settee had curtains around the lower part of it, which thus concealed him from sight. He said the Rebels passed right by him, and he heard them wondering if there were any Yankees in the house. They did not go any further than the hall and soon returned to the cellar. He assured us that he took a good, long sigh of relief after they had gone down and out, the way they came in.

This soldier was Corporal Michael O'Brien, of Co. A., 143rd Pennsylvania Volunteers, 1st Corps. He enlisted at Wilkesbarre, Pa., and at the time of the visit referred to above, was a resident of Waverly, Tioga County, N. Y. He said he had been wounded during the first day's engagement, by a ball striking him in the back, and then passing to his right arm, shattering it at the elbow. We all took occasion to examine his arm, and found it wasted away almost to the bone.

Another of the five wounded was a captain

of the 6th Wisconsin regiment, but his name
I do not know.

This is all the account I am able to
give of the Union soldiers concealed, nursed
and protected in our house during the battle.

Mother always called them her boys, and
often wondered what had become of them. It
may be that Corporal O'Brien was the only
one of them who survived the war.

———

Through the night of the first day of the
fight, my father was frequently up in the
garret; and from the window looking out
toward the Cemetery Hill, could distinctly hear
our troops chopping, picking and shoveling,
during the silent hours. Our men were busy
forming their line of breastworks, preparatory to
meeting the enemy on the morrow.

At different times while the battle was
going on, my father, accompanied by some of
the soldiers in the house, went to the garret
in order to look at the fighting out on the
hill.

While thus viewing the battle, they noticed, on one occasion, in the garret of the adjoining neighbor, a number of rebel sharpshooters, busy at their work of picking off our men in the direction of Cemetery Hill.

The south wall of this house, had a number of port holes knocked into it, through which the Rebels were firing at our men. All at once one of these sharp-shooters threw up his arms, and fell back upon the garret floor. His comrades ran quickly to his assistance, and for the time being, they appeared greatly excited, and moved rapidly about. A short time afterward they carried a dead soldier out the back way, and through the garden.

On account of this position occupied by the rebel sharpshooters, a continual firing was drawn toward our house ; and to this day no less than seventeen bullet holes can be seen on the upper balcony. One of the bullets cut a perfectly even hole through a pane of glass. The back porch down stairs, the fences and other places, were also riddled ; showing how promptly and energetically the Union boys replied, when once they detected the whereabouts of the enemy.

The greatest wonder is, that our men did not send a shell into that house, after they detected the rebel firing.

The sharpshooters on this part of the field, had their headquarters on the north of our house; it being at the nearest corner to the line of battle, and served as quite a protection to them.

At night, when all the folks had gone up stairs, these sharpshooters would enter the cellar in search of eatables. On these occasions, as was observed from the windows above, they carried milk and cream crocks, preserves, canned fruit, etc., out into the side street; and seating themslves on the pavement, and along the gutter, no doubt had an enjoyable feast, and a hilarious time over the provisions they had captured. They did not call it stealing in war times.

One day these same men, wanted my

mother to come up out of the cellar, and cook for them. She most positively declined; saying she would not dare to do it for her own family at such a time, and much less would she do it for them.

Had she complied with the request, she very likely would have lost her life; for it was just about that time, that bullets were passing through the kitchen, over and around the stove. Bullets came through the south side of the room, striking, and sometimes passing through the opposite side. Had anyone been standing in front of the stove or near it, they would have been in the line of the deadly missiles, and death would have been almost certain.

———

During the first day's battle, and after our men had retreated, a little girl was standing at the second story window of the house opposite ours. She had the shutters bowed, and was looking down into the street at the confusion below. Suddenly a shell struck the

wall just beside the shutter, tearing out a
large hole and scattering pieces of brick, mortar
and plastering all around the room in which
the little girl was standing. It entered and
struck some place in the room, rebounded and
fell out into the street.

Another ball is now placed in the wall,
to mark the place where the first one struck.
I am here reminded of the fact that many
persons while walking or riding past this place,
and having their attention called to this shell
sticking in the wall, neatly encased in brick
and mortar, think that it has been there just
as it arrived on the first day of the battle.
Shells were not quite so tidy in introducing
themselves at that time.

The little girl who had the narrow escape
referred to, was Laura Bergstresser, a daughter
of the then Methodist minister at Gettysburg.
She is now deceased.

So terrified was she at what had happened
that she ran over to our house for safety.
The soldiers in the house told her that it

was a stray shot and might never happen again. Being assured that she was just as safe at her own home, she ran back to her parents.

When this shell struck, a brother of the little girl, lay in a room close by, very low with Typhoid fever. Through the open doors he saw it enter and go out of the building.

———

It was Saturday morning, after the battle, when there was a ring of the front door bell. It was the first time the bell had rung since the conflict commenced. No one ventured out on the street during those three days, fearing that they might be picked off by sharp-shooters. Hearing the ringing, mother said :

" Oh ! must we go and open the front door ? " For she thought the battle would again be renewed. They however opened the door, and to their surprise the Methodist minister stood before them. He exclaimed :

" Don't you think the rascals have gone ?"
Father was so overjoyed, that not taking

time to consider, ran out just as he was, intending to go to the Cemetery Hill and inform our men of the good news.

He had gone about half a square from the house, when, on looking down, saw that he was in his stocking feet. He thought to himself: " No shoes! No hat! No coat! Why, if I go out looking this way, they will certainly think that I am demented!"

He turned to go back, and while doing so saw a musket lying on the pavement. He picked it up, and just then spied a Rebel running toward the alley back of Mrs. Schriver's lot. Father ran after him as fast as he could and called: " Halt!"

The fellow then threw out his arms, and said:

" I am a deserter! I am a deserter! " To which father replied:

" Yes, a fine deserter you are! You have been the cause of many a poor Union soldier deserting this world; fall in here. " He obeyed; and as father was marching him toward the house, he spied two more Confederates coming out of an adjoining building, and compelled them to "fall in."

These also, claimed to be deserters; but the truth is, they were left behind, when Lee's army retreated. He marched the three men out to the front street, and as there were some Union soldiers just passing, handed his prisoners over for safe keeping.

He then went into the house; put on his shoes and hat; took his gun and went up to the alley back of our lot. There he saw a Rebel with a gun in hand, also trying to escape. Father called on him to halt. The fellow faced about, put his gun on the ground, rested his arms akimbo on it, and stood looking at him. Father raised his musket, and commanded: "Come forward, or I'll fire!"

The Confederate immediately came forward and handed over his gun. On his way to the front street with this prisoner he captured two more and soon turned these over to our men.

Father then examined his gun for the first time; and behold! it was empty.

———

A few days after the battle, several soldiers came to our house and asked mother if she would allow them to bring their wounded Colonel to the place, provided they would send two nurses along to help wait on him, saying they would like to have him kept at a private house.

As we had a very suitable room she consented.

The wounded officer was carried to the house on a litter, and was suffering greatly. After they got him up stairs, and were about placing him on the bed, it was found to be too short, so that the foot-board had to be taken off and an extension added. The Colonel was a very tall man and of fine proportions.

He had been severely wounded in the right ankle and shoulder, the latter wound extending to his spine.

The surgeons at first wanted to amputate his foot, saying it was necessary in order to save his life ; but the Colonel objected, and said that if his foot must go he would go too.

Mother waited on him constantly, and the nurses could not have been more devoted.

He was highly esteemed by all his men, many of whom visited him at the house, and even wept over him in his suffering and help-lessness. They always spoke of him as one of the bravest men in the army.

Before long his sister came, who with ten-der care and cheering words no doubt hastened his recovery.

Several months elapsed before he was able to be removed ; when, on a pair of crutches, he left for his home in St. Paul. As he was leaving the house he could hardly express fully, his thanks and appreciation of our kind-ness ; and on parting kissed us all, as though he were bidding farewell to his own kith and kin. We, on our part, felt as though one of our own family were leaving. He promised that whenever able he would come back to see us.

About three years after the battle, I was standing on the front pavement one day, when a carriage suddenly stopped at the front door. A gentleman alighted, came up to me, shook hands, and kissed me without saying a word. I knew it was the Colonel by his tall, manly form.

He ran up the front porch, rang the bell, and on meeting the rest of the family, heartily shook hands, and greeted mother and sister with a kiss.

We were all glad to meet each other again, and we earnestly desired him to stay. He however, said his time was limited, and friends were waiting in the carriage to go over the battlefield. So we were forced to again say farewell.

The officer of whom I have just written, was Colonel William Colvill, of the First Minnesota Regiment. At the present writing his residence is in the city of Duluth, Michigan.

It was during the terrible struggle out by the Wheat Field, toward the close of the second day, when the confusion of the battle was confounding; when the contending columns had become mixed with each other on account of the dense smoke, when one of Wilcox' Regiments came unnoticed in contact with Humphrey's left, that General Hancock orders Colonel Colvill to " Forward " with his regiment.

The encounter is a desperate one. Many of the brave First Minnesota are slain in the hand to hand struggle; but the enemy is driven back with losses equally severe. During this engagement the Colonel received the wounds to which I have referred.

I have since learned, that out of 262 men comprising this regiment at Gettysburg, but 47 remained after this daring charge.

When Colonel Colvill and his attendants left our house, one of the men who had been nursing him, presented me with a gun and bayonet, saying :

" I bought it with my own money, and I give it to you ; and if any one comes after it, and wants to take it from you, just tell them that the gun was bought and paid for by the soldier who gave it to you."

One of the nurses was Milton L. Bevans, musician of Co. F, 1st Minnesota Regiment, now of Hamline, Minn. ; the name of the other, and the one who gave me the gun and bayonet was Walter S. Reed, private, Co. G, also of the same regiment.

―――

Some weeks after they had left, a Provost Marshal was sent to the town, to collect all arms and accoutrements belonging to the Government.

Some one informed him, that there was a gun at our house, for it was not long before two soldiers called. I suppose I had been bragging too much about my relic.

On going to the door, they asked me whether we had a musket about the house.

I said : " Yes sir ; but it is mine."

They replied that the Provost Marshal had sent them after it, and that they would have to take it.

I told them what the soldier who gave it to me had said; whereupon they expressed their sorrow, but added, that they would have to obey.

In my indignation at this treatment I said:

"If they are mean enough to take the gun they can have it; but it is *my* gun."

They seemed sorry as they rode away with my highly prized treasure, and I have no reason to doubt their sincerity.

About two hours after this, I happened to go to the front door, and on looking up the street, I saw the same two soldiers returning on horse back, one of them having a gun on his shoulder.

I ran into the house, and told my sister that I actually believed they were bringing back my gun.

Instantly the bell rang, and I told her that I was ashamed to go to the door, after talking to them the way I had.

So my sister went; but the soldiers said they wanted to see me.

I went to the door and found these same men looking quite pleased as they said to me:

" The Provost Marshal heard you were such a good Union girl, he has sent back your gun, and we are very happy to return it to you."

After attempting to apologize for the way I had addressed them, they said they did not blame me in the least for they knew how I must have felt at losing a gun obtained in the way I had this one. I still have it. On its stock are cut the initals P. L. W T., a custom quite prevalent in the army. I need hardly state how greatly I prize this relic.

I have also in my possession an officer's sword and scabbard which were presented to my sister just after the battle, by a soldier named Barney M. Kline of Company C, 55th Ohio Regiment. The scabbard must have been hit by a bullet or piece of shell, as it was almost broken off near the middle. This sword and scabbard he picked up in our orchard along

the Taneytown road, which place is now em-
braced in the National Cemetery.

———

For many weeks after the battle my thoughts
and attention were directed to the General Hospital, located about one mile east of the town.

This was a large collection of tents, regu-
larly laid out in Camp style.

As we passed along the Camp streets we
could look into the open tents, and behold
the row of cots on either side. Upon these
couches lay the sufferers who, a short while
before, had endured the terrors of battle, and
were now hovering on the verge of Eternity.

Here also were established the Christian and
Sanitary Commissions, ever exerting their moral
and humane influences. In their large tents,
was contained almost everything that Christian
civilization could suggest to meet the necessities
of those who had suffered in the conflict.

As is known to many of my readers, the
province of the Sanitary Commission was to
provide more especially for the bodily wants ;

whilst that of the Christian Commission, besides supplying necessaries for the body, took an earnest interest in the welfare of the souls of the wounded and dying. The many blessings derived from these adjuncts to our army, may not be fully known now, but they shall be revealed hereafter.

Prior to the formation of this general hospital, each corps had its own, in the locality where it had fought. This was on account of the convenience in promptly gathering and caring for its wounded. After the number of patients had become reduced, these hospitals were discontinued, and each corps was assigned to its section in the general hospital.

Many sad and touching scenes were here witnessed. Many a kind and affectionate father; many a fond and loving mother; many a devoted wife faithful unto death; many a tender and gentle sister, wiped the moisture of death from the blanched forehead of the dying hero, as they eagerly leaned forward to catch the last message of love, or to hear the announcement of a victory greater than that of death.

The friends and relatives who came to minister to the wounded were, on account of the crowded condition of the hotels, compelled to ask accommodations from private citizens. In this manner quite a number were taken into our home. Most of their time was spent at the hospital, some coming back to us in the evening, and leaving as soon as possible the next morning.

I was frequently invited to accompany these visitors, and in this way often found myself by the bedside of the wounded.

One lady who was stopping at our house, I remember in particular; a Mrs. Greenly. Her son lay suffering at the hospital, and in company we frequently visited him.

One day when he was very low it was concluded that by amputating his limb his life might be spared. After the operation had been performed her son sank rapidly. At last came the words : " *Mother! Dear Mother! —— Good bye!—— Good ——! Mother!* "——and all was over. Her darling boy lay before her in the embrace of death ; but a mother's tender love had traced a peaceful smile upon his countenance. As the life went out from that racked body hope and joy forsook that fond mother's heart.

Oh ! that sad face and bleeding spirit, as she bade us farewell to follow the coffined remains to her far off home.

Who will dare to say that with such sacrifices upon our country's altar our national inheritance is not sacredly precious ?

I shall never forget the anxious suspense of that mother. Whilst absent from her loved one, even for a few hours, her spirit knew no rest, and as soon as possible she would hurry back.

———

During our visits to the hospital, we became acquainted with individual soldiers. These received our special sympathies and attentions, hence our return was always looked forward to with cheering anticipations.

Having heard what they would be allowed to
have, when we again returned we brought them
such delicacies as were prescribed and which
they seemed most to crave. Our baskets were
filled with lemons, oranges, cakes, jellies, rolls
and other edibles. They always seemed glad
to look upon the flowers and bouquets which
we invariably brought along. Many of their
tents were decorated on the outside with wreaths,
festoons, corps badges wrought in evergreen,
and many other beautiful designs.

Our visits cheered the poor fellows, and
their eager requests to " come back again soon,"
made us feel that we were of some use even
in our feeble way.

Many of the town ladies would spend their
time in reading to the wounded. This seemed
to take their thoughts from their sad condition
and centre them upon objects more comforting
and delightful.

Frequently we attended religious services at
the hospital and gladly joined in the singing.
I have no doubt the soldiers fully appreciated

our presence and the part we took in the exercises ; for it must have made them think of their dear ones at home, and caused them to realize that they were once more among their sympathizing sisters of the North.

CHAPTER VIII.

CONCLUSION.

Years have come and gone since the happening of the events narrated in the preceding chapters, but they are as indelibly stamped upon my memory as when passing before me in actual reality.

The carnage and desolation, the joys and sorrows therein depicted, have all long since passed away.

Instead of the clashing tumult of battle, the groans of the wounded and dying, the mangled corpses, the shattered cannon, the lifeless charger and the confusion of arms and accoutrements, a new era of joy and prosperity, harmony and unity prevails. Where once the bloody hand of Mars blighted and killed the choicest of Nature's offspring, there Peace, with her smiles and arts has transformed the desolation into a Paradise of beauty and bloom. Where once I saw a terrible chaos I now behold a pleasing order.

The struggle between human bondage and universal freedom, the desire to destroy this government and dishonor her flag, the cruel hatred of Americans toward each other, no more blurs our fair land.

On the very spot where in their blindness they shed the blood of fratricide, I have seen the Blue and the Gray clasp hands, and in the presence of their fellow countrymen and before High Heaven, pledge their devotion to each other, and to a renewed and purified government. On this memorable ground I have seen Gens. Longstreet, Gordon, Hooker, and Sargt. Jones (who bore the colors of the 53d Virginia, in Pickett's charge, being thrice wounded ere he fell), with many others of the Gray, standing together with Gens. Sickles, Slocum, Beaver, Curtiss and others of the Blue; and like men and true patriots freely forgive and mourn the past.

I have heard them as representatives of different parts of our land, unitedly raise their voices in thanking God that we were once more a united people with one common cause.

To enter into detail concerning the present appearance of the battle-field is not my desire. It must be seen and studied to be appreciated. Who ever can, should not fail to visit the place.

Annually it is becoming more and more beautified. The positions of the several corps and regiments are marked by the finest sculpture of which art and science are capable. Avenues are opened so that the visitor can pass all along the line of the terrible conflict and at the same time learn from the inscriptions on the beautiful monuments, who were engaged, and at what period of the battle.

The National Cemetery, wherein repose the heroic dead, has become a marvel of loveliness. Baptized with the blood of patriots, dedicated in the immortal words of Lincoln nurtured and guarded by a grateful people, this spot for all time to come cannot be other than the nation's shrine of American virtue, valor and freedom. Here will posterity receive the same inspiration that prompted their ancestors to dare, to do and to die, for the perpetuity of the inestimable blessings that shall have come down to them.

What has been done and is still doing on the battlefield of Gettysburg, shows how devoted is the heart of the American nation to the memory of those brave men, who through their loyalty were willing to suffer and to lay down their lives in order that the precious institutions of our land might not perish.

What in my girlhood was a teeming and attractive landscape spread out by the Omnipotent Hand to teach us of His goodness, has by His own direction, become a field for profound thought, where, through coming ages, will be taught lessons of loyalty, patriotism and sacrifice.

From this combined volume of nature and art, mankind will learn that human freedom and Christian civilization have ever the smiles of a kind and allwise Providence.

Studying the annals here exhibited we cannot fail to learn that: " The God of battles " is ever present, that on those memorable days at Gettysburg " *The hand of our God was upon us, and He delivered us from the hand of the enemy.*"

THE END.

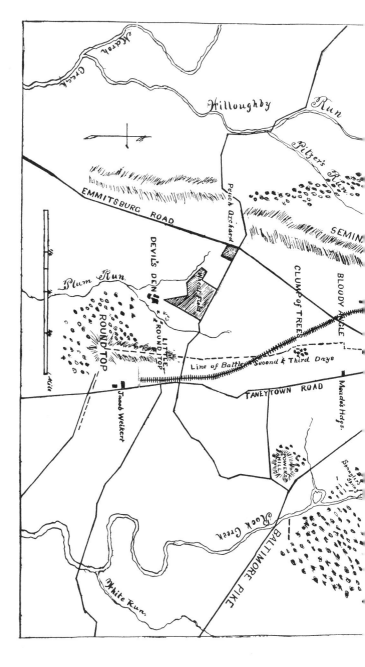